HOW TO LOSE YOUR FEAR OF FLYING

BY PERRY LAFFERTY

PRICE/STERN/SLOAN

Publishers, Inc., Los Angeles

1980

ILLUSTRATIONS BY ED POWERS

Copyright© 1980 by Perry Lafferty
Published by Price/Stern/Sloan Publishers, Inc.
410 North La Cienega Boulevard, Los Angeles, California 90048

ISBN: 0-8431-0654-9
Library of Congress Catalog Card Number: 80-80153

THOUGHTS AND ACKNOWLEDGMENTS

I had first thoughts for this book about a year after I took up aviation. It seemed that everyone who knew me wanted information about what goes on "up there," why I was involved in such a "dangerous" hobby, why they were either afraid or petrified of flying and so forth. I discovered that some married couples took separate planes when they traveled. Other acquaintances were frightened enough to spend three and a half days on a train from L.A. to New York rather than fly.

From time to time, when friends discussed their trepidations about a forthcoming flight, I would sit them down and do my best to explain why their fears were, to coin a phrase, "groundless." I'd talk about how an airliner works, the pilots are trained and checked, airlines are maintained, ground controllers operate, and on and on.

To my surprise, more often than not, these former "nonbelievers" would call after their trip to tell me how well everything went.

"I remembered what you said about turbulence, and when the bumps started they didn't bother me at all!" one exclaimed.

I finally decided that - as far as commercial aviation is concerned - what people don't know **does** hurt them.

So, if you are a nervous airline passenger, the following pages are intended to help. After all, flying is here to stay and is not only the fastest and most efficient way to travel, it is extraordinarily safe.

I'd like to acknowledge with thanks the cooperation of the Jeppesen Company in allowing the reproduction of certain charts and plates. Because some of these are navigational aids and are constantly being updated, the ones in this book are not to be used for navigation.

A number of people helped in the preparation of this book and I thank them all: Wayne Garrison, Chief of the Los Angeles F.A.A. Air Carrier District Office and his staff members - James L. Menard, Stoddard Baird, Dave Barr and Wythe Fielder; also D.F. Kirkpatrick of Western Airlines, Corky Kronshage of the Air Transport Association and Captain Barry Schiff of TWA.

My wife and family were extraordinarily supportive in this effort. As was my secretary, Cary Straatsma, who practically became a pilot herself from typing the manuscript a dozen times.

And, last but not least, I must thank Jon Kodani, Jim De Long, Tony Pavolinis, Skip Feher and Larry Battersby, who not only taught me how to fly, but how to love it.

NOTE TO THE READER

What you don't know about flying **may** be hurting you.

How do you feel about it? Nervous, a little anxious, even downright panicky? If so, why? Because of the tragic accident in San Diego in fall of 1978 or the one in Chicago in spring of 1979? Or because of the large number of small planes that never seem to make it home?

This book is designed to lighten the spirits of the tense air traveler by stating the **facts** about flying. Like this one: **In 1978, the last year for which figures are available, the commercial airlines completed 99.99991% of their flights without a fatality.**

Or: **General aviation (small planes) comprises 96% of all pilots flying 98% of the civil aircraft 84% of the total hours over 61% of the aircraft miles.** With this in mind, the accident rate in small planes becomes extremely small, doesn't it?

So, if you are nervous about taking an airline flight, just read on. What you learn should turn a potentially nerve-wracking experience into a pleasurable one.

Q: HOW MUCH COMMERCIAL FLYING IS DONE EACH YEAR?

A: In 1978, the latest year for which complete figures are available, the National Transportation Safety Board and the Aircraft Owners and Pilots Association reported that the certified route air carriers flew over two and a half **billion** miles (2,797,000,000 to be exact). Translated into hours, this equals 6,783,000.

Q: THAT'S A LOT. HOWEVER, EXACTLY WHAT WAS THE FATALITY RATE?

A: The fatal accident rate per **million aircraft miles** flown was .0021 – or .088 per 100,000 aircraft **hours** flown.

Q: HOW SAFE ARE THE AIRLINES COMPARED TO LIGHT GENERAL AVIATION AIRCRAFT?

A: The comparative safety of airlines and general aviation is difficult to assess. One large commercial aircraft carrying a lot of people on a long flight will accumulate many "passenger miles." A small plane, which carries fewer people shorter distances, must fly more often to accumulate an equal number of passenger miles. So a comparison using passenger **miles** is disadvantageous to general aviation.

On the other hand, because there usually are more fatalities when a larger airplane has an accident, a comparison based on **fatalities** is disadvantageous to commercial airlines.

Perhaps the one base which most accurately reflects a comparison of airline and general aviation safety relates fatal accidents to the number of flights. This, after all, is the concern of individuals. "If I get into an airplane, what are my chances of getting down safely?"

In the last year for which complete figures are available, **airlines conducted 99.99991% of their** flights with no fatalities, as was stated earlier. **General aviation completed 99.99904% of its flights with no fatalities.**

Included in the general aviation figures are suicides, test flying, and some of the more hazardous operations such as low-level crop treatment, helicopter construction work and stunt shows.

In summary, the difference between safety of general aviation and the airlines, using the base of fatal accidents to number of flights, is minimal.

Other bases may be used to show other results. Paramount in this comparison of airline and general aviation flights is the tremendous safety record of all air transportation.

Q: WHAT PERCENTAGE OF TRANSPORTATION-RELATED ACCIDENTS INVOLVE FLYING?

A: Here are the transportation fatalities for 1978:

		Total	Percentage
Highway		50,145	(91.0 %)
Passenger cars	28,120		
Pedestrians	7,920		
Pickup Trucks & Vans	5,950		
Motorcycles	4,500		
Heavy Trucks	1,010		
Pedalcycles	890		
All others	1,755		
Grade Crossings		1,064	(1.9 %)
Railroad		632	(1.4 %)
Intercity: crew, pedestrians and others	569		
Intercity passengers	13		
Rapid Rail Transit	50		
Boating		1,500	(2.7 %)
Commercial	179		
Recreational	1,321		
Aviation		1,709	(3.1 %)
General	1,548		
Air Carrier	161		
(nearly all in San Diego crash)			
Pipeline		33	(0.06%)
TOTAL TRANSPORTATION FATALITIES		55,083	(100.00%)

Q: HOW MANY PASSENGERS WERE CARRIED?

A: In 1978 scheduled airlines in the U.S., including international flights but excluding charter flights, carried 274,719,000 passengers.

Q: I CAN'T EVEN IMAGINE HOW ONE OF THOSE GIANT AIRPLANES FLIES, LET ALONE HOW IT GETS OFF THE GROUND IN THE FIRST PLACE.

A: Ask 25 people why an airplane flies and you'll get 25 different answers, most of them wrong. Without getting too technical, here is a simple explanation.

A scientist named Bernoulli discovered that the **faster** fluid moves through a pipe the **less pressure** it exerts on the pipe. This principle was was applied to the airplane wing. Most wings are designed so that the top surface is slightly **curved** and therefore **longer** than the bottom surface, which is flat. Consequently, when the plane is moving through the skies the air must travel a **greater distance** across the curved top of the wing than it does across the flat bottom. Naturally, it must take the same amount of **time** for the air to move across both the top and the bottom. Since the air flowing across the top of the wing must move **faster** to travel the greater distance in the same time, it exerts less pressure on the wing top than does the air traveling across the wing bottom.

Therefore, the air which is moving across the wing **bottom** at a **slower speed** exerts **more pressure,** and, as a result, holds up the wing. Of course, you need some engines and a few other things, but this is the general idea.

Q: COULD YOU FIRST GIVE ME SOME OVERALL AIRLINE ACCIDENT STATISTICS?

A: Certainly. The following are through the courtesy of the Aircraft Owners and Pilot Association.

Aviation Accident Rates – 1978	Airlines
Total accidents	26
Accidents with fatalities	6
Accident rates per 100,000 aircraft hours	
Total	0.3687
Fatal	0.08849
Fatalities	2.3746
Accident rates per million aircraft miles	
Total	0.0089
Fatal	0.0021
Fatalities	0.0575
Accident rates per 100,000 departures	
Total	0.40
Fatal	0.08
Fatalities	0.32
Flights completed without fatality	99.99991%

Q: HOW MANY AIRPLANES ARE THERE IN THE ENTIRE U.S. AIRLINE AND GENERAL AVIATION FLEET AND HOW FAR DID THEY FLY IN 1978?

A: Active Aircraft - 1978

General Avaition		198,800	(98.9%)
Propeller	184,700		
Jet	5,500		
Rotorcraft	5,000		
Other	3,600		
Air Carrier		2,263	(1.1%)
Propellor	21		
Jet	2,242		
Rotorcraft	3		
		201,063	(100.0%)

12

Q: THE MAJOR AIRPORTS TODAY ARE SO BUSY. HOW DO THEY KEEP THE AIRPLANES SEPARATED?

A: A "Terminal Control Area" has been established at major airports with heavy traffic.

A diagram of the one at Los Angeles appears on the next page. Note the left side of the diagram $\frac{70}{40}$E and $\frac{70}{20}$C for example. This means unless directed from the ground by a radar controller, **no** plane may enter the airspace between 4,000 and 7,000 feet in the first example, and between 2,000 and 7,000 feet in the second. Los Angeles airport is located in the middle of the diagram. Note its runways in the center "square." You will see that to the left and right of the runways no airplane traffic may enter the airspace between the **surface** and up to **7,000 feet** without permission from the ground controllers. This, of course, protects jet approaches and departures.

Terminal Control Areas presently exist in Los Angeles, Atlanta, Chicago, Boston, Dallas, Miami, New York, San Francisco, Washington D.C., Cleveland, Denver, Detroit, Houston, Kansas City, Las Vegas, Minneapolis, New Orleans, Philadelphia, Pittsburgh, Seattle, St. Louis and San Diego. The establishment of others is now being contemplated.

Q: HOW MANY PILOTS ARE THERE IN A JETLINER?

A: It depends. On the big ones (707s, DC-8s, certain 727s, 747s, DC-10s, L-1011s) a Captain, a First Officer (co-pilot) and a Second Officer (flight engineer) fly the airplane. On most airlines the flight engineer is also a

LOS ANGELES TERMINAL CONTROL AREA (GROUP 1)

Effective date: September 16, 1971

CEILING 7000' MSL

70/20 — 70 C — — Ceiling of TCA in hundreds of feet MSL
— — Letters identify areas
— — Floor of TCA in hundreds of feet MSL
(Floors vary according to area)

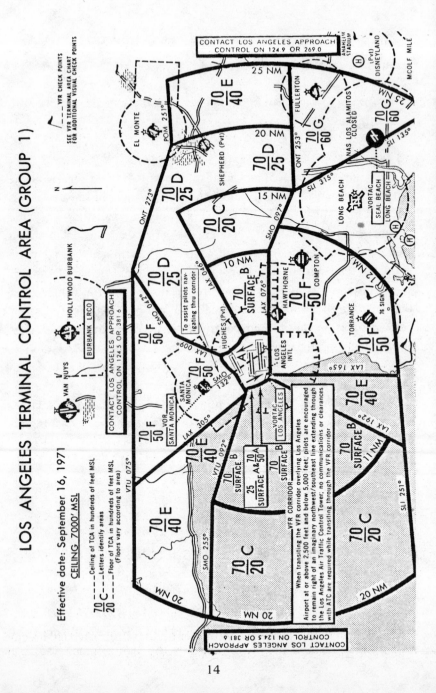

qualified pilot. On the smaller jets (737s, DC-9s, BAC-111s) there are just a Captain and a First Officer. If necessary an airliner can be landed by just one pilot.

Q: HOW MANY PARACHUTES DO THEY CARRY ON JETLINERS?

A: None.

Q: WHY NOT?

A: The primary reason is weight. People who parachute-jump as a hobby have, in addition to their main 40-lb. parachute, a second ("safety") chute. If you got rigged up with all this gear you'd never get into the restroom.

Q: HOW DOES THE GOVERNMENT SUPERVISE THE OPERATION OF THE AIRLINES?

A: There is a series of extensive Federal Aviation Administration (F.A.A.) regulations which apply to the air carriers. They spell out **everything** from weight limitations to aural warning devices for landing gears.

In the field there are several Air Carrier District Offices which directly supervise the activities of the airlines. These offices employ, among others, operations inspectors who work with airline management in evolving training procedures; airman certification inspectors who act as check pilots for all flight crew members (they ride in the cockpit); maintenance inspectors who cooperate with top management of the carriers in setting up various standards; and avionics inspectors, the "black box boys" who see that all the complex radio and navigation equipment is kept in tip-top shape.

Q: JUST HOW WELL MAINTAINED ARE COMMERCIAL AIRLINERS?

A: Very well. A complete maintenance program following stringent regulations is worked out for each type of aircraft between the plane's manufacturer, the airline and the F.A.A. which is charged with its supervision. In recent months many of the inspection procedures have been intensified. Following is a typical example of maintenance performed on a Western Airlines DC-10:

1) A Turnaround Inspection:
This is performed at maintenance stations prior to the origination of a flight. The logbooks and the maintenance releases for the aircraft are reviewed and a "walkaround" of the plane is performed by mechanics.

2) A Termination Service Inspection:
This is also done at maintenance stations on all terminating flights where the plane is on the ground for at least four and a half hours. A more involved series of checks is performed in this series. One of them might be checking tire pressures, for example.

"A" Check - Every few months, which is still more extensive.

"B" Check - more and more complex, is done at 1,000 hours.

"C" Check - very, very detailed - at 3,000 hours of flight time.

3) The Structural Inspection Major.
This check is performed at 21,000 hours and is just what its name indicates.

Between the 1,000-hour and 21,000-hour checks there are many other inspections (4,000, 6,000, 8,000, etc.) in which certain items are examined on a progressive basis.

Q: WHOEVER HEARD OF A JET AIRLINER FLYING 21,000 HOURS?

A: Some of the bigger airline jets fly an **average of 12 hours a day,** day in and out. That's about 350 hours a month, or 4,200 a year. So, it would take just about **five years** to rack up 21,000 hours.

Q: WHAT REQUIREMENTS MUST MECHANICS MEET TO WORK ON COMMERCIAL AIRLINERS?

A: There aren't enough pages in this book to list the types and specialities of maintenance personnel, supervisors and training procedures involved in keeping a big jet flying. Suffice it to say that a "Certificated Mechanic" must have attended a government-approved school and must have had 18 months experience in power plants, or 18 months in airframes, or a combination of 30 months total just to get his ticket. Two and a half years!

This basic training **might** be enough to get a mechanic hired by an airline which then commences its **own** endless training program.

Q: HOW MANY REGISTERED PILOTS ARE THERE AMONG THE 220,000,000 PEOPLE IN THIS COUNTRY?

A: As of 12/31/78, nearly................................800,000. Of these, slightly more than 200,000 were students.

(a) **Private Pilot Certificate**............................337,644
These pilots are involved in general aviation, principally pleasure and some business flying.

(b) **Commercial Pilot Certificate**.......................185,833
To get one of these you must have at least 250 hours flight time and fulfill more involved government requirements (including the requirement for an instrument rating).

(c) **Airline Transport Rating**............................55,881
This is the highest rating a pilot can get and requires at least 1,500 logged hours plus the passing of many written, oral and practical tests.

(d) Helicopter pilots 4,874

(e) Glider pilots and lighter-than-air 9,727

Employed by certificated U.S. scheduled airlines 28,336

Total Active Women Pilots as of 12/31/78
(almost all in general aviation) 49,874

Q: HOW MANY TAKEOFFS AND LANDINGS ARE MADE EACH YEAR?

A: At airports with F.A.A. towers during 1978:

General aviation (small planes)	51,664,261
Airlines	10,214,440
Air taxi	3,883,099
Military	2,532,068
Total takeoffs and landings	68,293,868

Q: WHICH AIRPORTS HAVE THE MOST TRAFFIC?

A: The 10 busiest airports with F.A.A. Control Towers in 1978 were:

Airport	Total Takeoffs & Landings
1. Chicago O'Hare	760,613
2. Long Beach, CA.	617,363
3. Santa Ana, CA.	604,169
4. Van Nuys, CA.	601,230
5. Atlanta	556,992
6. Los Angeles	541,942
7. Opa Locka	500,491
8. Oakland	466,957
9. Denver	466,645
10. San Jose	463,027

Incidentally, small general aviation airports such as California's Santa Ana, Van Nuys, Long Beach and San Jose have such heavy operation counts because of the extremely high number of **private planes** in that state (the highest density airspace in the world). JFK in New York as well as La Guardia are ranked in the next 10 busiest. Worldwide, London's Heathrow Airport takes the overseas prize for the largest number of operations.

Q: ARE THERE ANY LIMITATIONS ON HOW MUCH FLYING AN AIRLINE CREW CAN DO?

A: Absolutely. Regulations dictate that a crew member can fly no more than 1,000 hours in any calendar year (a 40-hour week comes out to about 2,000 hours), no more than 100 hours in any calendar month, no more than 30 hours in any seven consecutive days.

Q: CAN ANY AIRLINE CAPTAIN FLY ANY ROUTE SEGMENT SERVED BY HIS COMPANY?

A: No. Not until he has been qualified as directed by F.A.A. regulation 121.443.

Q: WHAT RATING DO AIRLINE PILOTS HAVE?

A: It's called an Air Transport Rating for which the F.A.A. regulations require that the applicant must demonstrate very extensive aeronautical knowledge and ability.

Q: SO THERE'S A FLIGHT TEST FOR SOMEONE WANTING TO SECURE AN AIR TRANSPORT RATING (ATR)?

A: There certainly is. The requirements that a candidate must meet are extensive, including having a **minimum** of 1,500 hours in his logbook.

Q: ONCE THE PILOT HAS HIS AIR TRANSPORT CERTIFICATE, IS HE ALL SET?

A: I'm afraid not.

This is merely a **certificate** stating that certain tests have been passed. In order to be hired by an airline, the pilot must next go through an additional series of training schedules demanded by government regulations. Then the pilot must be **specifically instructed** for the type of airplane to be flown.

Q: THEN THE GOVENMENT SETS UP REQUIREMENTS FOR THE TRAINING OF AIRLINE FLIGHT PERSONNEL?

A: F.A.A. regulations (Part 121) specify the content of the general training program, how it should be conducted and the minimum hours involved.

For instance, pilots must be re-trained for each **new type** of airplane to which they are assigned. The training schedule includes ground school, simulator time and the like. One normal progression is to begin as a second officer (flight engineer) on a three-engine 727 jet which uses a three-person crew. After some years, he or she moves up to second officer (co-pilot) on a two-engine Boeing 737 or a DC-9 which uses just a pilot and a co-pilot. Years later he or she can be promoted to **captain** of the 737 or DC-9. **Each move means additional training.**

When the transition to a larger airplane (707, DC-8, L-1011, DC-10, 747) is made, the pilot is put through intensive additional instruction in the new equipment.

Regulations further state that a captain must come back for **recurrent training every six months,** a co-pilot every year.

Q: WHAT IS INVOLVED IN BECOMING AN AIRLINE CAPTAIN?

A: Becoming the captain of an airliner operated by a major carrier is one of the most difficult job goals imaginable. Before a candidate can even be employed as a flight engineer (the usual entrance position), he or she is subjected to a battery of tests administered over a period of several months. These include written, oral and practical examinations designed to test knowledge, reflexes and psychological makeup.

The candidate for a cockpit position who passes these comprehensive tests must still compete with the many others applying for the few, highly sought-after job opportunities with the airlines.

Most of those fortunate enough to be hired can look forward to at least 10 years with the line before becoming a captain. On the jumbo jets it's not uncommon to find captains in their 50s with over 20,000 flying hours in their logbooks.

To be a captain on an airline you have to want it **really bad.**

Q: SOME PEOPLE PREFER ONE AIRLINE OVER ANOTHER. ARE THERE ANY SIGNIFICANT DIFFERENCES BETWEEN DOMESTIC AIRLINES?

A: Only in the way they paint their planes, meals they offer, or how polite and efficient their ticket agents are. As far as aircraft types are concerned **there is absolutely no difference.** A 707 owned by one airline is serviced and operated by the same rules (set down by the manufacturer and supervised by the govenment) as 707s on every other airline.

Q: WHEN I ARRIVE AT AN AIR TERMINAL A HALF-HOUR BEFORE MY FLIGHT, IS THE CREW OF MY PLANE ALREADY ABOARD?

A: Probably, if the flight is leaving on time. They use this time for the pre-flight check lists we'll talk about later.

Q: DOES A PILOT ARRIVING AT THE AIRPORT GO RIGHT TO THE AIRPLANE?

A: Hardly. About an hour before departure he goes to the Dispatch Office. There he is given computerized information concerning the status of the flight (when it will be leaving, from which gate, etc.).

Q: WHAT NEXT?

A: Each trip is **planned** by a dispatcher who creates a document called a **flight release**. This is the legal authority to operate a specific flight. Before picking up this release the pilot studies the weather (more on this later). He then signs the form which makes it legal for him to command this particular flight. **No flight may operate without an executed flight release which actually is a joint agreement between the dispatcher and the pilot as to the safety of the operation.**

Q: YOU SAID IT WAS PLANNED BY THE DISPATCHER?

A: That's right. **But the captain must agree with it.**

Q: WHAT'S INCLUDED IN THIS FLIGHT RELEASE?

A: It tells the captain the maximum weight at which the airplane can be operated, the minimum fuel that's allowed, what the alternate airport is, and the route to be followed.

Q: WHAT IF WE GO THROUGH SOME CLOUDS RIGHT AFTER OUR TAKEOFF? HOW CAN WE BE SURE WE WON'T RUN INTO A SMALL AIRPLANE INSIDE THEM?

A: No airplane, large or small, is allowed inside a cloud of **any** size **unless it's on an instrument flight plan** and **being controlled from the ground**. The pilots of all airplanes under VFR (Visual Flight Rules) are responsible for keeping separation between themselves and other planes. However, those on an instrument flight plan (including jet airliners and some small planes) will also be given advisories about other traffic by the ground controllers.

Q: WHAT EXACTLY IS AN INSTRUMENT FLIGHT PLAN?

A: It's simply a form printed by the government which asks questions about the captain's intended route. He fills in, among other things, the numbers of the jet airways he intends to travel that day, how long the trip is expected to take, the desired altitude and expected time of arrival. This instrument flight plan is usually coded at the takeoff airport and teletyped to the nearest Air Route Traffic Control Center (ARTCC), where it is stored in a computer until the plane is nearly ready for takeoff. At that point, on request of a departure controller, the computer retrieves and activates it.

At this point, the flight plan is put on teletype to the various airports and stations along the jetliner's route and to the approach controllers at its destination and alternate airports (in case the weather should go below minimums).

It's like a letter you might write to a friend in Los Angeles saying you plan to leave St. Louis on a certain day, drive to L.A. on Interstate 10, and arrive at a certain time.

A simplified version of a high-altitude flight plan would look like this:

FL 250 ALB J37 ATL J14 BHN.

Translation: Requesting to fly at 25,000 feet from Albany, New York, via Jet Route 37 to Atlanta, Georgia and Jet Route 14 to Birmingham, Alabama.

The ARTCC computer sorts out the flight plan from other aircraft requesting the same routing and altitude at this approximate time, and decides whether to approve or amend the captain's request. It might, for instance, approve everything but the altitude requested. The flight might be sent to 31,000 feet if too many planes are scheduled for 25,000 feet that day and time. Or, the computer might route the flight slightly differently, via other jet airways from Albany to Birmingham.

Q: DOES THE DISPATCHER MAKE HIS OR HER OWN FLIGHT PLAN IN ADDITION TO THE FLIGHT RELEASE?

A: Yes. An additional flight plan is prepared utilizing a central computer. A wide variety of information concerning a particular leg of a trip (or, on a non-stop transcontinental flight, the **whole** trip) has been programmed into it. The computer already has the current weather and the altitudes available for use. These two elements will determine much of what is to come.

A portion of an actual flight plan from Portland to Los Angeles is shown on the opposite page. It is too complex to explain in detail. However it includes the amount of fuel needed for the trip. That figure is reached by calculating fuel needed for taxiing to the runway, takeoff and climbout, cruising, descent, reaching an alternate airport (in case the planned destination is unusable), and landing reserve. It also lists indicated airspeed, temperature, wind speeds, estimated time to fly each leg, and the total time for the trip. Because the weight of an airplane is so critical, fuel is always listed in **pounds** rather than gallons.

On the flight plan shown, the plane will burn 800 pounds of fuel just taxiing to the runway. In the climbout, 5,710 pounds will be burned. Total for the trip from Portland to Los Angeles will be 16,930 pounds of fuel burned. **Incidentally, all weights are predicated on the loss of one engine**.

Q: IS THERE ANY WAY THAT AIRLINE SECURITY PEOPLE CAN SPOT POTENTIALLY DANGEROUS PASSENGERS?

A: In cooperation with the federal government, most airlines have developed something called "A Profile of a Suspicious Person." Exactly what this is remains restricted information, but the profile procedures have proven extremely effective in the weeding out of potentially dangerous individuals. The system operates from check-in time right up to the boarding of the plane.

```
PDX-LAX ROUTE B  0748  PDX J67 LKV J5 TIOGA FAT FAT 158RAD/98
   DME
   DERB LAX
   RTE INFO. .206 LKV. .182 RNO. .96 TIOGA. .65 FAT. .199 LAX
   -03/M-
FL NM MT MACH IAS  T  WC  TAS GS  ZT  T/T   ZBO   AXBO  ACNM
                                    0800   000800
CLB 0144    340/M780 P09 P029 385 414 021 0021 05710 006510 0144
RNO
330 0244    M810/288 P05 P022 476 498 029 0050 04090 010600 0388
TOD
330 0245    M810/288 P05 P000 476 476 031 0121 04330 014930 0633
LAX
DNT 0115    M810/350 P10 P010 363 373 019 0140 02000 016930 0748
NBFL 370
REQUEST AIREPS PVER CHECKPOINTS ABOVE
LGT/PSBL MDT CAT CLB    FRNT
LGT CAT VCNTY 50N RNO    RIDGE AND FAT    TROF
OCNL LGT CAT DONT    FRNT
PDXLAX   . .ARVL MUST BE WITHIN 15 MINS OF SKED IN TIME
            SHOWN ON RELEASE TO COUNT AS ON TIME FLT
   FP WT RAMP 141813/LNDG 134883 NAM 0723 PSGR 094
TRIP TIME/BURN    PDX LAX   140/016930    -TAXI 10/1811
IFR/ALTN    BUR            010/002500
RESERVE                    006500  SKED OUT 1715GMT
HOLD TIME/BURN            010/001580    SKED IN 1913 GMT
BLOCK FUEL                   027510
MGL    171/4 LWL
:9A9646 111836
A15BB 411
```

Q: WHO IS THAT MAN I'VE SEEN WALKING AROUND THE PLANE BEFORE TAKEOFF AND WHAT IS HE DOING?

A: He's the second officer, sometimes referred to as the flight engineer. He checks the plane visually for structural integrity and general airworthiness. He reviews the condition of the tires and checks the pressures of the various systems, plus a number of other items.

Q: AFTER THE FLIGHT ENGINEER HAS FINISHED HIS WALK-AROUND INSPECTIONS, WHAT DOES HE DO DURING THE REST OF THE FLIGHT?

A: Big jet airplanes have many systems that must be monitored during flight. These include the electrical system, the hydraulic system (which operates landing gear extension and retraction and other controls), and one of the most important, the fuel system. While the pilots are doing the actual flying, the flight engineer is constantly checking to see that these systems are operating properly. He keeps an especially keen eye on the amount of fuel being consumed, making periodic estimates for the captain.

Q: IS THE FLIGHT ENGINEER ALSO A PILOT?

A: In almost every case he is. However, a small minority of airlines does not have this requirement.

Q: WHAT HAPPENS IF THE FLIGHT ENGINEER ISN'T A PILOT AND SUDDENLY A SECOND PILOT IS NEEDED?

A: Flight engineers are found only on planes that also use a pilot and a co-pilot. In the rare event that one pilot should become incapacitated, the other can handle the aircraft.

Q: SOMETIMES BEFORE TAKEOFF YOU CAN SEE THE PILOTS IN THE COCKPIT READING. ARE THEY REVIEWING INSTRUCTIONS FOR THE FLIGHT?

A: No. they are going over their checklists. **Each type of plane has a different one** which covers every aspect of its operation. These lists are many pages long and are followed meticulously **before, during and after every flight.**

Q: WHILE TAXIING TO THE RUNWAY WHAT DOES IT MEAN WHEN THE PILOT ASKS: "WILL FLIGHT ATTENDANTS PLEASE PREPARE THEIR DOORS FOR DEPARTURE?"

A: Prior to takeoff, an arming mechanism is locked into place on each door of a jetliner by the attendants. In the event that the plane must be evacuated in a hurry, all anyone has to do is unlatch the door. This will cause big chutes to automatically deploy under the doors. Passengers can jump into them and slide the distance from the plane to the ground. This height can be anywhere from 10 to 20 feet depending on the aircraft.

Q: WHAT ABOUT AVIATION WEATHER?

A: Weather reports and forecasts are available to airline pilots in many forms. Meteorology is a complicated business so we won't expect you to understand it all. We'll just hope to give you a glimmer of some of the various tools that are available.

For example, on the facing page is an "Explanantion of a Weather Station Model and Symbols." It may be indecipherable to you, but it gives the jet captain a lot of important information.

Q: IS THERE ONE SINGLE MAP AN AIRLINE CAPTAIN CAN REFER TO WHICH SHOWS WHERE THE BAD WEATHER IS?

A: Yes. An example is on page 34 and is called a "U.S. High Level Significant Weather Prognosis Chart." It indicates areas and the degree of turbulence as well as icing conditions. It also gives the altitudes where turbulent conditions are forecast to occur. (Add two zeros to the numbers given to show the altitudes.)

Q: WHO COLLECTS WEATHER DATA FOR AVIATION USE?

A: Weather service is a joint effort of the National Weather Service (NWS), the F.A.A., the military weather services and other aviation

EXPLANATION OF WEATHER STATION MODEL AND SYMBOLS

At Weather Bureau offices, maps showing conditions at the earth's surface are drawn 4 times daily or oftener. The location of the reporting station is printed on the map as a small circle. A definite arrangement of the data around the station circle, called the station model, is used. The station model is based on international agreements. Thru such standardized use of numerals and symbols, a meteorologist of one country can use the weather maps of another country even though he does not understand the language. An abridged description of the symbols is presented below.

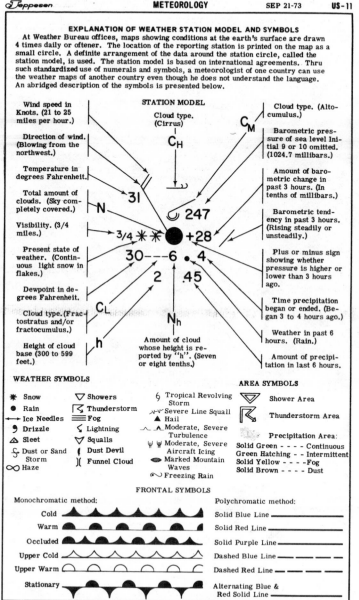

U.S. High Level Significant Weather Prog. (400 – 70 mb)

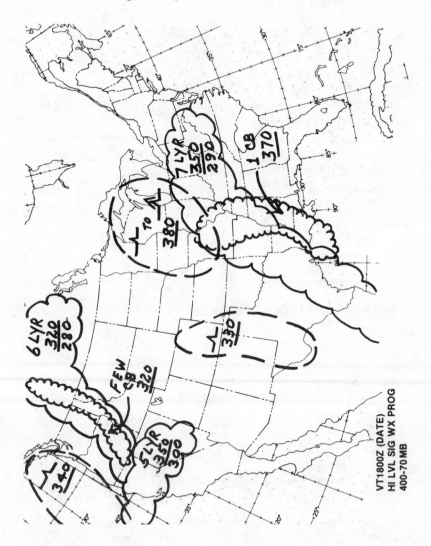

groups and individuals. Because of international flights and a need for worldwide weather information, foreign weather services also provide vital input into our service.

Q: WHAT KINDS OF DRUGS, PRESCRIPTION OR "OVER-THE-COUNTER" VARIETIES, ARE FLIGHT CREWS ALLOWED TO TAKE BEFORE THEY FLY?

A: Absolutely none, The only exception, and it's rare, is when a prescription has been specifically written by a flight surgeon. Included in this prohibition are such everyday substances as antihistamines, Tylenol and cough medicines.

Q: ARE THERE ANY OTHER PROHIBITIONS FOR PILOTS?

A: They can't scuba dive for 24 hours prior to a flight.

Q: WHY?

A: Because scuba diving can be dangerous, particularly if a person has been diving to depths for any length of time. Under the increased pressure of the water, excess nitrogen is absorbed into the system. If sufficient time has not elapsed prior to takeoff in order to allow a person's system to rid itself of this excess gas, a pilot may experience "the bends" at altitudes under 10,000 feet.

Q: WHAT IF THE CAPTAIN HAS BEEN DRINKING PRIOR TO A FLIGHT?

A: F.A.A. regulations require that no member of an air carrier flight crew drink alcohol for 24 hours before a flight. If this rule is violated, it could result in loss of a pilot's license.

Q: CAN AN AIRLINER BE OVERLOADED BEFORE TAKEOFF?

A: No. The weight limitations of all airliners have been carefully analyzed and set down during their design phase and are **never** exceeded. In most cases computers are used to make load determinations.

Q: SOMETHING ALWAYS SEEMS TO GO WRONG AFTER YOU ARE ABOARD AND SEATED. IT'S VERY NERVE-WRACKING!

A: An airliner is an extremely complex piece of equipment; it undergoes all sorts of **continuing inspections,** most of them long before you board the flight. Two of the most important of these are (1) the flight engineer's "walk-around" prior to starting up the engines and (2) the checklist routine that the pilot and co-pilot go through. Both procedures are designed to triple- and quadruple- check the airworthiness of the plane for that particular trip.

Most of the problems discovered at this time are of a very minor nature. However, the policy of all airlines and their captains is that **everything** must be operating **by the book** or they won't even leave the ramp area.

Q: ARE THE OXYGEN MASKS THE FLIGHT ATTENDANTS ALWAYS TALK ABOUT BEFORE TAKEOFF REALLY IMPORTANT?

A: They certainly are. If a jetliner should experience a massive decompression at 35,000 feet (the times this has happened through the years can be counted on your fingers), a person without oxygen would lose consciousness in a matter of minutes. Should this situation ever arise, just put the mask on and relax. And don't be disturbed that the pilot is making a rapid descent. He's just getting you down to where the air is thicker so you won't need the mask anymore.

Q: ARE THERE MASKS FOR EVERY PASSENGER?

A: Yes.

Q: WHAT IF SOMEONE IS CARRYING AN INFANT IN A SINGLE SEAT?

A: The flight attendant will bring a portable oxygen unit which will be used in addition to the regular oxygen mask.

Q: HOW HIGH CAN A PERSON FLY BEFORE THE USE OF OXYGEN IS REQUIRED?

A: In an **unpressurized** aircraft (jets are all pressurized) the regulations require that oxygen be available for all passengers above 14,000 feet.

Q: HOW DOES A CAPTAIN GET INFORMATION ON THE AIRPORT SCHEDULED AS HIS DESTINATION?

A: Besides weather information, the Airman's Information Manual lists complete details on every airport in America. (See opposite page). The dispatcher also has detailed information.

DIRECTORY LEGEND SAMPLE

CITY NAME

§ **AIRPORT NAME** (ORL) 2.6 E GMT−5(−4DT) 28°32'43"N 81°20'10"W **JACKSONVILLE**
113 B S4 **FUEL** 100, JET A OX 1, 2, 3 TPA—1000(800) AOE CFR Index A Not insp. **H-4G, L-19C**

IAP

(18)► **RWY 07-25:** H6000X150 (ASPH) S-90, D-160, DT-300 HIRL
RWY 07: ALSF1. Trees. **RWY 25:** REIL. Rgt tfc.
RWY 13-31: H4620X100 (ASPH) HIRL
RWY 13: VASI—GA 3.3° TCH 89'. Pole. **RWY 31:** VASI—GA 3.1° TCH 36'. Tree. Rgt tfc.

(19)► **AIRPORT REMARKS:** Attended 1200-0300Z‡. LLWSAS. Acft 100,000 lbs or over ctc Director of Aviation for
approval (305) 894-9831. Fee for all airline charters, travel clubs and certain revenue producing acft.

(20)► **COMMUNICATIONS: ATIS** 127.25 **UNICOM** 123.0
NAME FSS (ORL) on fld 123.65 122.65 122.2 122.1R 112.2T (305) 894-0861
®**NAME APP CON** 124.8 (337°-179°) 120.15 (180°-336°)
TOWER 118.7 **GND CON** 121.7 **CLNC DEL** 125.55 **PRE TAXI CLNC** 125.5
®**DEP CON** 124.8 (337°-179°) 120.15 (180°-336°)
STAGE I SVC ctc ORLANDO APP CON

(21)► **RADIO AIDS TO NAVIGATION:** VHF/DF ctc PHOENIX FSS
NAME (H) VORTAC 112.2 ORL Chan 59 28°32'33"N 81°20'07"W at fld. 1110/8E
VOR unusable 050-060° beyond 5000'
HERNY NDB (LOM) 221 OR 28°30'24"N 81°26'03"W 067° 5.4 NM to fld.
ILS 109.9 I-ORL Rwy 07. LOM HERNY NDB
ASR/PAR

(22)► **COMM/NAVAID REMARKS:** Emerg frequency 121.5 not available at tower.

39

Q: CAN THEY MEASURE THE HEIGHT OF THE CLOUDS OVER THE AIRPORT?

A: Absolutely, by using a little gadget called a **rotating ceiling beam ceilometer**. A complete explanation is on the opposite page.

Q: AFTER THE CAPTAIN HAS GONE THROUGH THE FLIGHT RELEASE WITH THE DISPATCHER AND THE CHECKLISTS WITH HIS CREW, IS HE READY TO TAKE OFF?

A: Sort of, but there's a lot more to it. During the completion of the pre-flight and the first portion of the checklists, one of the cockpit crew contacts a controller with the title of "Clearance-Pre-Taxi." This special ground control position is found only at the larger airports serving commercial traffic. The crew member gives the flight number and destination and asks that the flight plan be activated. The clearance controller puts the request into the computer by teletyping the nearest Air Route Traffic Control Center and indicating that such-and-such flight is ready.

Next, the captain switches his radio to another frequency to contact the **ground** controller from whom he receives permission to taxi from his gate location to the assigned runway. By the time the plane is nearing the runway, the flight plan clearance has been received from the center, confirming the **specific departure procedure,** routes and altitudes for the trip. It's at this point that the ground controller turns the plane over to the **tower** controller.

The tower controller (the person you always see in the movies) is the

ROTATING BEAM CEILOMETER

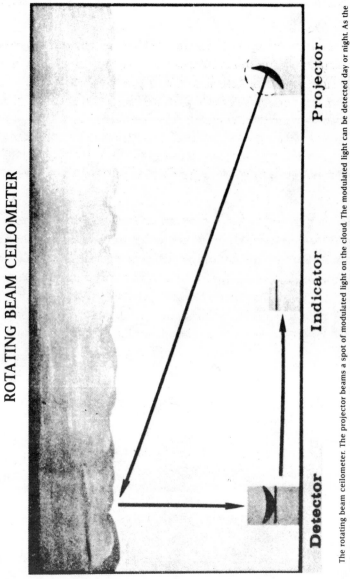

Detector **Indicator** **Projector**

The rotating beam ceilometer. The projector beams a spot of modulated light on the cloud. The modulated light can be detected day or night. As the projector rotates, the spot moves along the cloud base. When the spot is directly over the detector, it excites a photoelectric cell measuring the angle of the light beam. Height of the cloud is then determined automatically by triangulation. This instrument scans much more rapidly than the older fixed beam ceilometer which is being phased out.

one who actually releases the plane, saying: "Cleared for takeoff!" Moments after liftoff the tower controller will switch the jet to the **departure** controller on another radio frequency. This person has jurisdiction over the airspace within the vicinity of the airport up to an altitude of roughly 7,000 feet. The departure controller will steer the plane, keeping it separated from other aircraft as it is climbing out. The jet will finally be given to a **sector** controller at the nearest Air Route Traffic Control Center, who will monitor the flight until it starts to vacate his airspace. Then it is handed over to the **next** sector controller. On a flight from Los Angeles to New York, for example, this "handing off" process would happen every several hundred miles at altitudes from approximately 7,000 to 45,000 feet.

As the flight nears its destination, the air control process is reversed. It goes from center sector controller to approach controller to tower controller (who clears the plane to land) to ground controller, who clears it for taxi to the assigned gate.

Q: JUST BEFORE WE LEAVE THE RAMP THERE'S A PERSON OUT-SIDE ON THE GROUND MAKING HAND AND ARM SIGNALS TO THE PILOT. IS HE A SORT OF TRAFFIC COP?

A: In a way. He's a signalman. The captain needs his help because, unfortunately, these huge planes don't have rear view mirrors and he can only see in a forward direction and slightly to the side.

Modern jets are so huge they could easily bump into something on the ground without proper guidance. See diagram.

AIRPORT OPERATIONS
HAND SIGNALS

SIGNALMAN DIRECTS TOWING

SIGNALMAN'S POSITION

FLAGMAN DIRECTS PILOT TO SIGNALMAN IF TRAFFIC CONDITIONS REQUIRE

POINT TO ENGINE TO BE STARTED

ALL CLEAR (O.K.)

START ENGINE

PULL CHOCKS

COME AHEAD

LEFT TURN

RIGHT TURN

SLOW DOWN

STOP

INSERT CHOCKS

CUT ENGINES

NIGHT OPERATION
(Use same hand movements as day operation)

EMERGENCY STOP

Q: WHAT ARE SOME OF THE THINGS THAT DETERMINE WHETHER AN AIRLINER CAN TAKE OFF? YOU KNOW, LIKE FOG, RAIN OR SNOW.

A: Several important factors besides the weather minimums affect a commercial jet's clearance to "go." One of the most important is the **maximum allowable takeoff gross weight.** This maximum varies tremendously for any given airplane and is a computation based on several factors. The two most important are the **altitude at the airport** and the **temperature** on that particular day.

Take a Boeing 707. The absolute maximum takeoff gross weight allowable for this airplane **under the most ideal conditions** (a temperature of 59 degrees at sea level) is 331,600 pounds. The airport at Denver, Colorado, is a very good example of how altitude (about 5,000 feet above sea level) and temperature affect the 707's takeoff weight. **On a hot summer day** in Denver a 707 taking off cannot weigh more that **260,000 pounds.** In **mid-winter** at **zero** degrees, this same airplane would be allowed to take off weighing **320,000 pounds.** A difference of 60,000 pounds!

Whatever the maximum allowable takeoff gross weight for an airplane is, it is carefully computed **before each flight and is never exceeded.**

Q: OCCASIONALLY ON TAKEOFF I'VE SEEN FUEL LEAKING OUT OF THE WINGS. ISN'T THIS DANGEROUS?

A: That's not fuel, it's water. Under certain weather conditions condensation occurs, and when the plane starts to roll down the runway the air flowing over the wing causes this excess water to be blown off. It's like the condensation that forms on a car's windshield.

Q: THERE ARE TIMES WHEN A PILOT DECIDES TO GO BACK TO THE AIRPORT FOR LANDING RIGHT AFTER TAKEOFF. BUT BEFORE HE DOES THAT HE HAS TO DUMP SOME FUEL. WHY THE FUEL DUMPING?

A: Many jetliners have a certificated maximum gross **takeoff** weight which is **greater** than the gross weight for which they are stressed for **landing.** If the pilot wants to return, there are two possibilities: to fly around until the fuel burns off (which can take a while) or to dump it and get back down.

Q: SOMETIMES WHEN WE'RE ROLLING DOWN THE RUNWAY IT SEEMS LIKE THE PLANE WILL NEVER GET OFF THE GROUND. WHY?

A: The same jetliner on takeoff requires different runway lengths depending upon its weight, the elevation of the airport, outside air temperature, humidity and several other factors. All this data is computed prior to each takeoff and a liftoff speed is established for that particular run.

Q: WHAT HAPPENS IF AN ENGINE QUITS RIGHT AFTER THE PLANE HAS LIFTED OFF THE GROUND?

A: Nothing. All jets are certificated to be able to continue takeoff even in the event of an engine failure.

Q: HOW ABOUT TWO ENGINES QUITTING?

A: Two engines on a jet airplane seldom quit simultaneously because each operates on its own system. It is conceivable that an engine on a four-engine jet could throw a turbine blade which could cut in and stop the second engine on the same side, but the odds make this **extremely** unlikely.

Q: YOU MENTIONED THAT ALL THE WEIGHTS, INCLUDING TAKEOFF WEIGHT, ARE PREDICATED ON THE LOSS OF ONE ENGINE.

A: That's right, However, for **overwater** flights (New York to London, San Francisco to Honolulu, etc.), if the plane happens to lose **two** of its engines, it is designed to make it to land **even if this happens directly at mid-point over the ocean.** The 707, DC-8 and 747 have four engines each, so **if you lose two, you will still have two.** Wide-bodied DC-10s and L-1011s, on the other hand, have only **three** engines each, so by losing two you're left with **one.**

A DC-10 on takeoff for an overseas flight weighs approximately 440,000 pounds. If two engines go out at midpoint over the water, **it will fly safely back to land on one engine.**

Q: CAN A GROUND CONTROLLER WARN A PLANE IF HE OR SHE THINKS IT'S TOO LOW?

A: You bet. The controller will immediately issue an advisory to the pilot if he is aware that an aircraft is at an altitude which, in his judgment, places it in unsafe proximity to the ground or obstructions. He'd say something like: "Low altitude alert. Check your altitude immediately."

Q: WHAT ABOUT GETTING TOO CLOSE TO ANOTHER PLANE?

A: Same deal. Under these circumstances the order should be: "Traffic alert. Advise you turn right heading 100 degrees and descend to eight thousand feet immediately."

Q: NOW ABOUT WEATHER. DON'T GIVE ME ANYTHING FANCY. JUST TELL ME IN PLAIN ENGLISH WHAT TURBULENCE IS.

A: There are several different kinds of turbulence and several different causes for it. The various types of turbulence are, of course, simply bumps--some big ones, some bigger ones.

Look at it this way. You've seen pictures of a fisherman standing happily in his hip boots in the middle of a trout stream. You probably only noticed the expression on his face, happy or sad depending upon the number of fish that he's caught.

Next time take a look at the stream itself. You will note that, as water flows downhill, it must detour around or over the rocks in its path. Doing so, it burbles, turning into what is often described as "white water."

Turbulence is basically formed the same way. Wind flowing over a mountain range has its smooth flow interrupted. One stream of wind flowing into another that is coming from a different direction causes a double interruption to the smooth flow. In all these cases bumps occur because of interference to the flow. When an airliner enters these areas it gets jostled around.

Next time you hit some "rough air" think of a trout stream.

Q: WHEN WE HIT SOME TURBULENCE WHY DON'T I JUST SIT BACK AND RELAX?

48

A: Why don't you?

Q: WHAT HAPPENS IF A TIRE BLOWS OUT DURING TAKEOFF OR LANDING?

A: Usually nothing. A plane rides on many tires. Take a 747 for example: it has 18 tires, four trucks with four tires on the main landing gear, and two tires on the nose wheel.

Q: I'VE OFTEN NOTICED A GRINDING NOISE AND A LOUD "THUMP" RIGHT AFTER TAKEOFF AND JUST BEFORE LANDING. WHAT IS THAT?

A: The sound of the landing gear being retracted makes the grinding noise. The "thump" is the sound of the doors closing on the well where the wheels are stored (to streamline the plane for the enroute portion of the flight). Before a touchdown at the arrival airport, the captain puts the landing gear back down. More grinding. Also, perhaps a "thump" as the gear locks into place.

Q: HOW DOES THE CAPTAIN KNOW WHETHER THE LANDING GEAR IS DOWN? HE CAN'T SEE IT FROM WHERE HE SITS.

A: There are lights on his control panel which indicate whether the landing gear is up or down and locked into position.

Q: HOW DOES A CONTROLLER DECIDE WHAT RUNWAY A JET WILL USE FOR TAKEOFF AND LANDING?

A: As important as from what direction the wind is blowing (so that the controller can line the plane up on a runway which more or less points **into** the wind), is the **weight** of the airplane. The older runways are stressed to handle only 707s, DC-8s and the twin jets such as the 737 and DC-9. **Jumbo jets,** the 747, DC-10 and L-1011 (known as "heavies"), can take off and land only on runways which have been stressed to handle their additional weight. Also, the jumbo jets require a longer runway from which to takeoff than their smaller siblings.

Q: I'VE DEPARTED FROM THE SAME AIRPORT ON MANY DIFFERENT OCCASIONS. ONE TIME WE TAXIED RIGHT OUT AND TOOK OFF IN ABOUT THREE MINUTES. ANOTHER TIME IT SEEMED LIKE THE PILOT WAS DRIVING ALL OVER THE FIELD TRYING TO FIND THE RUNWAY. CAN YOU EXPLAIN?

A: The captain has a ground map of every airport he uses, so you may rest assured that he isn't lost. Note the taxi diagram for Denver's Stapleton Airport. The passenger concourses are located at the bottom left.

Since airplanes **always** take off and land **into** the wind (it gives them better lift), the captain will be directed by the control tower to the runway having the most favorable wind conditions.

If he was directed to Runway 35 L (left) adjacent to the terminal, you'd be on your way in no time (barring any other type of delay). However, if

50

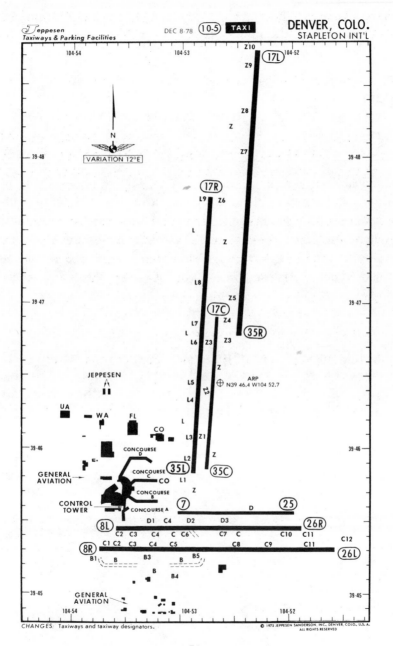

VARIATION 12°E

JEPPESEN

UA   WA   FL   CO   CONCOURSE D

GENERAL
AVIATION   CONCOURSE C   CO

CONTROL   CONCOURSE B
TOWER   CONCOURSE A

ARP
N39 46.4 W104 52.7

17L
17R
17C
35R
35L   35C
7   25
8L   26R
8R   26L

GENERAL
AVIATION

the prevailing wind favored Runway 17 L (at the very top of the diagram) it's a much longer taxi prior to takeoff. Over three miles, actually.

Q: JET CAPTAINS OR FLIGHT ATTENDANTS ARE ALWAYS TELLING US WHAT ALTITUDE WE WILL BE FLYING. WHY IS THAT?

A: Probably because they hope you'll find it interesting. Actually, the **most** fascinating thing about flight altitudes is that very definite rules exist about them. For example, during the **enroute phase,** all flights moving from **east to west** must fly **at even** altitudes: 34,000, 36,000, 38,000 and so on. Flights going **west to east** fly only at **odd** altitudes: 33,000, 35,000, 37,000 and on upwards, Obviously, this is a paramount safety feature.

Q: OFTEN THE FLIGHT ATTENDANT WILL SAY THAT HE OR SHE CAN ARRANGE FOR A RENTAL CAR AT THE DESTINATION AIRPORT. HOW DOES THE ATTENDANT GET IN TOUCH WITH THE RENTAL AGENCY TO MAKE THE REQUEST?

A: An inflight radio-telephone is available on certain aircraft. The flight attendant merely calls the air-to-ground operator, gives the appropriate number and places the order.

Q: DO YOU THINK IT'S A GOOD IDEA TO KEEP YOUR SEAT BELT FASTENED ALL THE TIME YOU'RE IN YOUR SEAT?

A: Yes. Including when the plane is taxiing.

Q: WHY?

A: Because it just isn't possible to forecast **every** bump that may be out there in the path of the plane, either in the air **or** on the ground.

Q: I KNOW IT'S VIRTUALLY IMPOSSIBLE TO HIJACK A UNITED STATES AIRLINER TODAY (WITH ALL THE SECURITY PRECAUTIONS IN EFFECT), BUT SUPPOSE SOMEONE DID. IF THE HIJACKER WOULDN'T ALLOW THE CAPTAIN TO USE THE RADIOS TO NOTIFY GROUND PERSONNEL WHAT WAS HAPPENING, WOULD THERE BE ANY OTHER WAY HE COULD ANNOUNCE HIS PREDICAMENT WITHOUT THE HIJACKER CATCHING ON?

A: Yes. There is a rather unobtrusive instrument in the cockpit panel called a "transponder." Without causing any undue suspicion on the hijacker's part, it would be relatively easy for the captain to dial a special four-number hijack code causing alarms to ring all over the place in various ground stations. The stations, in turn, would then track the flight wherever it is going.

Q: WHY IS THE COCKPIT DOOR ALWAYS KEPT LOCKED?

A: Government regulations require it. They also state that no one other than authorized personnel may enter the flight deck at any time. In addition, to minimize pilot interruption, most airlines have instituted their own rules prohibiting flight attendants from entering the cockpit or calling on the intercom during the takeoff and landing phases.

Q: I'VE SEEN PICTURES OF AIRLINE COCKPITS. WHAT ARE ALL THOSE INSTRUMENTS?

A: In addition to the electronic equipment used for communications and navigation, pilots have (among other things): an airspeed indicator which tells how fast the plane is going ("Indicated Airspeed"); a vertical speed indicator that tells the speed at which they are ascending or descending; an altimeter for reading the height above sea level; a radar altimeter that reads out the height above the ground, which they use on approach; and a magnetic compass. The cockpit also contains a directional gyro which gives the same information as the magnetic compass, but in an easier-to-read visual presentation; distance-measuring equipment that spells out nautical miles to a given point, the time to get there and how fast the plane is traveling **over the ground**. There is also an attitude indicator which gives a graphic picture of the plane's attitude (ascending, descending, turning, level flight), and many instruments which monitor the conditions of the engines and the amount of fuel remaining.

Q: I'VE OFTEN HEARD ABOUT AN "AUTOMATIC PILOT." WHAT IS IT AND HOW DOES IT WORK?

A: Simply put, an automatic pilot on an airliner is a series of computers programmed by the pilot. An airplane operates in three axes. Its nose can pitch up and down in the vertical axis. Its rudder (tail) can yaw from side to side in its lateral axis and it can roll from side to side on its horizontal axis. Basically, what the automatic pilot does is to sense whenever the plane starts the smallest deviation from the altitude or the heading that the pilot has "cranked in," and automatically corrects the error.

It has several even more sophisticated features, like being able to lock onto a "glide slope" or fly a "descent profile". It's a very safe, efficient device that reduces cockpit fatigue and allows for uninterrupted flight planning while a trip is actually in progress.

It can instantly be disconnected by simply touching a button attached to the pilot's control yoke.

Q: WHAT HAPPENS WHEN AN AIRLINE CAPTAIN UNEXPECTEDLY FLIES INTO A THUNDERSTORM?

A: Let's first define a thunderstorm. A thunderstorm is composed of a series of "cells" and is generally local in nature. It is invariably produced by cumulonimbus clouds (the big black towering ones) and is accompanied by lightning and thunder.

With today's sophisticated weather radar systems, airline captains rarely fly into thunderstorms unexpectedly. It is possible, by using these radar readouts, for an airliner to pick its way through squall lines of thunderstorms and to avoid the cells which give the big trouble.

However, in the general vicinity of thunderstorms some turbulence can be expected although it doesn't **always** materialize.

Q: WHAT WOULD HAPPEN IF A JETLINER WAS STRUCK BY LIGHTNING?

A: Nothing much. There would be a blinding flash followed by a very big "bang", and then silence. If, after landing, you were to accompany the ground crew on its post-flight inspection, you would probably discover a tiny hole about the size of a dime where the lightning actually touched the plane. Incidentally, after touching the aircraft, it passes right on through and goes its merry way.

Q: EXACTLY WHAT IS AN AIRWAY?

A: A high altitude airway might be compared to an interstate highway. Both run across a large section of the United States. On page 58 is a section of an instrument high altitude chart with the jet airways clearly marked. Note at the top left of the chart, is Spokane, Washington. If the captain wanted to fly to Great Falls, Montana (top right), he would file jet airway J136 to Mullan Pass then jet airway J36 to Great Falls.

Q: HOW ARE THOSE "HIGHWAYS IN THE SKIES" MADE UP? AFTER ALL, THERE AREN'T ANY ACTUAL ROADS.

A: Much cross-country flying on instruments is done via radio navigation stations called "Very High Frequency Omni Ranges" (VOR)

There are literally hundreds upon hundreds scattered throughout the United States. Each one acts something like a lighthouse sending out a radio signal which sweeps around a 360 degree circle. VORs also transmit another signal which goes out simultaneously in **all** directions at once. There is a VOR receiver in the airliner cockpit which sorts out the two signals. It tells the pilot that the VOR station is either ahead of or behind him, and whether it's off to the right or the left.

HIGH ALTITUDE CHART

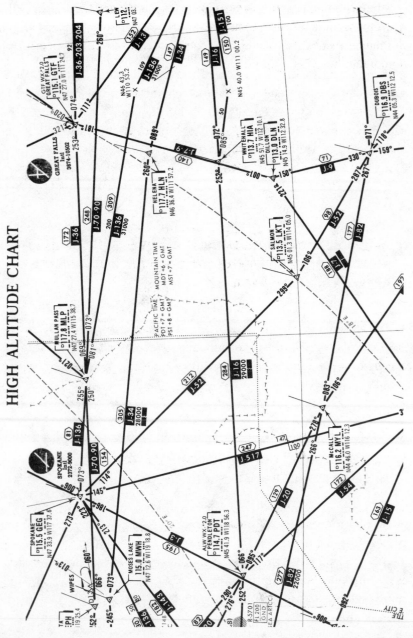

When the pilot is on the correct course for a particular airway, the instrument indicates it. Jetliners also use something called an Inertial Guidance System. It is a self-contained navigation unit which requires no contact with the ground.

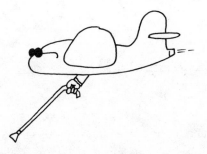

Q: IF TWO JETS ARE FLYING IN THE SAME DIRECTION AT THE SAME ALTITUDE ON AN ENROUTE AIRWAY, HOW FAR ARE THEY KEPT SEPARATED FROM ONE ANOTHER?

A: The ground radar controllers, using their radar scopes to indicate the position of each airliner, keep them separated from each other by between five and ten miles, depending upon the type and size of the planes.

Q: I'VE READ THAT THE CONCORDE AND SOME OF THE MILITARY PLANES FLY AT "MACH" SPEEDS. WHAT IS MACH?

A: A Mach number is the relationship between an aircraft's true air speed and the speed of sound. A plane traveling at Mach 1.6 means that it's going .6 faster than the speed of sound. A Concorde cruising between New York and London at 55,000 feet at Mach 1.6 will be traveling approximately 920 miles per hour. Incidentally, the temperature up there is **minus** 59 degrees.

Q: CAN THE CAPTAIN SEE OTHER PLANES ON A RADAR SCOPE?

A: No. Jetliners carry weather radar only. Separation of planes on instrument flight plans is the function of the ground controllers.

Q: SHOULD I WORRY ABOUT GETTING AIRSICK?

A: If you don't worry about getting airsick you probably won't. Unlike ocean liners (or even sailboats), which are subject to slow, monotonous, unrelenting rocking that can upset the most stalwart of stomachs, airliners (when in turbulence) don't follow any set pattern of bumps. Consequently, air sickness is much less common than sea sickness.

Q: THERE ARE MANY MILITARY AIRPORTS ACROSS THE UNITED STATES. IN CASE OF AN EMERGENCY WOULD OUR JETLINER BE PERMITTED TO LAND AT ONE OF THEM?

A: In case of emergency **any** plane can land at **any** airport.

Q: WHAT HAPPENS IF AN ENGINE SHOULD CATCH ON FIRE DURING FLIGHT?

A: Let's take an engine on a 707. First the pilot "retards the throttle" (like taking your foot off the accelerator in your car). Next, he activates a lever called a "fire pull" which shuts off all liquids to that particular engine. Finally, he has two fire bottles in each engine which he uses singly. If the first one doesn't extinguish the blaze, the second one certainly should.

Q: WHAT HAPPENS IF BOTH THE PILOTS GET FOOD POISONING AT THE SAME TIME AND PASS OUT?

A: The pilot and the co-pilot of an airliner never eat the same meal prior to takeoff or in the air. The odds that they would both get food poisoning from **different** meals are probably a million to one.

Q: BUT WHAT IF THEY SHOULD BOTH GET DEATHLY SICK FOR SOME OTHER REASON? VIRUS OR LEGIONNAIRE'S DISEASE?

A: Diseases like those don't come on in a flash. There usually is some hint that a person is coming down with something. A pilot won't fly if he doesn't feel well. A big part of his job is to be sharp, alert and ready to handle whatever may happen.

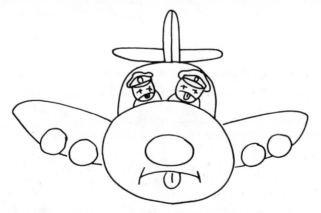

Q: SPEAKING OF FOOD POISONING, WHY ISN'T AIRLINE FOOD BETTER?

A: Sorry, this book's not about that.

Q: I REALLY GET CRAZY WHEN I LOOK OUT THE WINDOW IN ROUGH AIR AND SEE THE WINGS SORT OF FLAPPING UP AND DOWN. WHAT KEEPS THEM FROM BREAKING OFF?

A: If they didn't "flap" up and down they might do just that. Think of it this way: if you had no shock absorbers on your car, imagine what a bumpy ride you would get and how hard it would be on your automobile. The "flapping" motion of the wings absorbs some of the bumps in the air just like your shocks do on the ground. Because the wings sort of "roll with the flow" there's virtually no chance for them to sustain structural damage.

Q: IF A PASSENGER IS SUDDENLY TAKEN SERIOUSLY ILL, HOW DOES THE CAPTAIN DETERMINE TO WHICH AIRPORT THE FLIGHT WILL BE DIVERTED?

A: The captain asks the ground controller handling the flight about the weather conditions at the airport chosen as being the most ideal for landing. If conditions permit, that's where the plane will go. If there is a weather problem the captain and the controller will work out an alternate.

Q: IF A 747 LOST ALL FOUR OF ITS ENGINES AT ONCE WOULD IT DROP LIKE A ROCK?

A: On the contrary. Without power, a 747 descends on a slope of three degrees, allowing it to glide (depending upon various conditions) 15 to 18 feet **forward** for each **one** foot it descends. If a pilot in a 747 lost all four engines at 37,000 feet, he could glide 140 miles **in any direction**. Repeat, **in any direction**. This means he or she would have a choice of landing spots within a **62,000 square mile area**.

To put it another way: a 747 over Daggett, California, at 37,000 feet could easily glide to Los Angeles, a distance of approximately 120 miles.

Q: DO BIG PLANES OFTEN LOSE ALL THEIR ENGINES AT ONCE?

A: It's virtually unknown. Airline pilots I've talked with had trouble coming up with more than two or three cases - and they usually were the same ones.

Q: I HATE IT WHEN WE GET PUT INTO A HOLDING PATTERN IN THE CLOUDS FOR AN HOUR JUST BEFORE WE'RE SUPPOSED TO LAND. WHY IS THIS DONE?

A: Don't worry. A holding pattern is simply a flight course in the shape of a racetrack. The ground controller assigns an incoming airplane to the **top** of the stack as he releases the airplane on the bottom of the stack to depart for the airport and land. Every plane in between the top and bottom planes is separated from all others by an altitude of 1,000 feet at all times. All planes are instructed when to descend and begin another racetrack pattern 1,000 feet below their **previously** assigned altitudes.

The diagram on the opposite page gives a detailed set of rules for pilots to follow when executing what are called "Timed Approaches From A Holding Fix." It is another way of doing what is described above. The diagram should help you to visualize what goes on in a holding pattern.

Q: OBVIOUSLY, AFTER THE CAPTAIN STARTS HIS DESCENT, IT'S NOT POSSIBLE TO CONTINUE USING THE "HIGH ALTITUDE JET CHART." WHAT THEN?

A: The high altitude jet charts are used by airliners flying between 18,000 feet above sea level and 45,000 feet. **Below** 18,000 feet, pilots use one of a series of **low** altitude charts. They serve the same purpose.

Section II: I. ARRIVAL-IFR (Cont'd)

TIMED APPROACHES FROM A HOLDING FIX   (Cont'd)

3.   Each pilot in an approach sequence will be given advance notice as to the time he should leave the holding point on approach to the airport. When a time to leave the holding point has been received, the pilot should adjust his flight path to leave the fix as closely as possible to the designated time.

Example:

The following illustration depicts a final approach procedure from a holding pattern at a final approach fix (FAF).

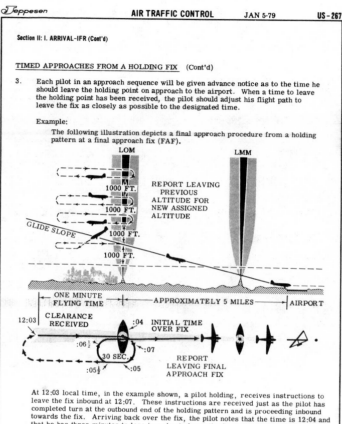

At 12:03 local time, in the example shown, a pilot holding, receives instructions to leave the fix inbound at 12:07. These instructions are received just as the pilot has completed turn at the outbound end of the holding pattern and is proceeding inbound towards the fix. Arriving back over the fix, the pilot notes that the time is 12:04 and that he has three minutes to lose in order to leave the fix at the assigned time. Since the time remaining is more than two minutes, the pilot plans to fly a race track pattern rather than a 360° turn, which would use up two minutes. The turns at the ends of the race track pattern will consume approximately two minutes. Three minutes to go, minus two minutes required for turns, leaves one minute for level flight. Since two portions of level flight will be required to get back to the fix inbound, the pilot halves the one minute remaining and plans to fly level for 30 seconds outbound before starting his turn back toward the fix on final approach. If the winds were negligible at flight altitude, this procedure would bring the pilot inbound across the fix precisely at the specified time of 12:07. However, if the pilot expected a headwind on final approach, he should shorten his 30 seconds outbound course somewhat, knowing that the wind will carry him away from the fix faster while outbound and decrease his ground speed while returning to the fix. On the other hand, if the pilot knew he would have a tail-wind on final approach, he should lengthen his calculated 30-second outbound heading somewhat, knowing that the wind would tend to hold him closer to the fix while out-bound and increase his ground speed while returning to the fix.

Q: SOUNDS LIKE A LOT OF CHARTS.

A: There is one more. It's called an **area chart**. These are furnished for areas **surrounding busy airports**. On the opposite page is a portion of the area chart representing the airways just east, south and north of Los Angeles Airport. If a jetliner was descending over Pomona (above the center of the chart) and was going to land at Ontario (to the right of center), it would be flying a Victor (low altitude) airway number V-197. Note that directly under the designation V-197 is the figure 4500. This means it isn't allowed to descend below this altitude on this particular route segment unless so instructed by the controller. The numbers 16 over V-197 tell the captain it's 16 nautical miles from Pomona VOR to Ontario VOR.

Q: WHAT HAPPENS IF THE WEATHER SUDDENLY GOES SOUR AT MY DESTINATION AIRPORT? WHAT PLANS HAVE BEEN MADE TO TAKE US SOMEWHERE ELSE?

A: First of all, the weather seldom goes sour **suddenly**. However, assuming that it happens, the F.A.A. requires that every plane carry enough fuel to get to its destination airport, **plus** enough for travel to its most distant alternate airport, **plus** a reserve of at least 45 minutes.

Q: IT MAKES ME VERY NERVOUS WHEN I THINK OF A PILOT LANDING A HUGE PLANE ON A RUNWAY THAT HE CAN'T EVEN SEE.

A: Oh, the pilot can see the runway - but not until the last few seconds. In most cases it works like this: the approach radar contoller on the

AREA CHART

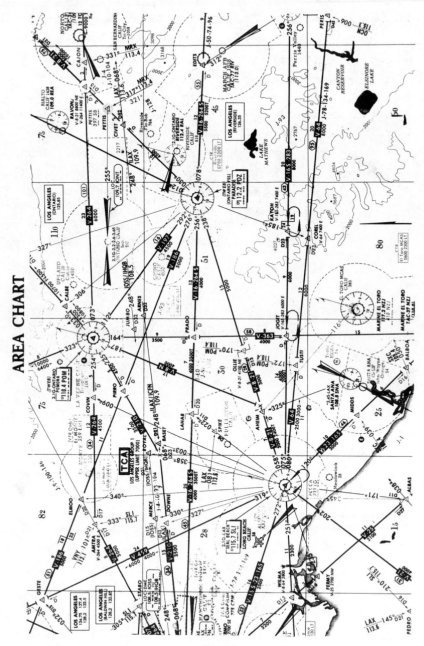

67

ground clears the airliner for approach to a certain runway. The captain steers the plane to the final approach after taking instructions from the controller to intercept a radio beam called a **localizer**. This is part of a precision approach called an Instrument Landing System. On the opposite page is an **approach plate** for the Instrument Landing System that your captain might use for runway 24L (left) at Los Angeles International Airport. In addition to the localizer radio beam, which is simply an extension of 20 to 30 miles of the centerline of the landing runway, there is another beam coming up called a **glide slope**. This radio beam tells the captain what descent angle to maintain on the way down. There are also some marker beacons along the course which give distance to the airport.

It's a remarkable system that allows most jets to descend to **200 feet** above the airport with only a half-mile of forward visibility.

Certain airliners have more sophisticated versions of this ILS which allow them to go down to 100 feet with almost **no** forward visibility restrictions. Today an Autoland System is in existence which does just what its name implies: it lands the plane automatically, with the pilot sitting nearby twiddling his thumbs. (This system has not yet been approved for full use in the United States.)

Probably in years to come these systems will become more and more automated. They will depend upon the **captain** as a backup instead of the other way around.

LOS ANGELES, CALIF.
LOS ANGELES INT'L
ILS Rwy 24L
LOC 108.5 IHQB
Apt. Elev 126'

ATIS Arrival 133.8

LOS ANGELES Approach (R)-See first apch chart for freq.

LOS ANGELES Tower N Complex 120.8

S Complex 118.9

Ground 121.75   Helicopter 119.8

MSA
OS LOM

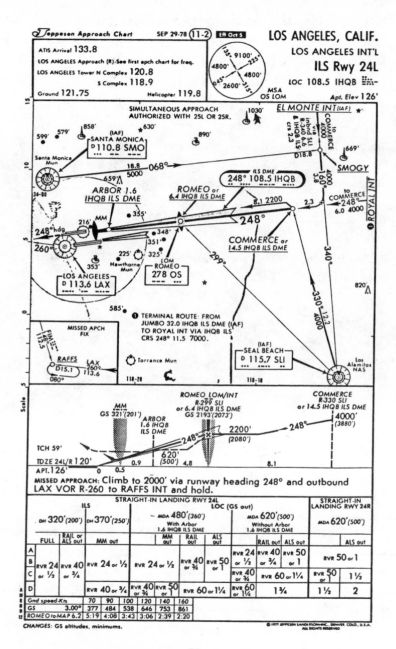

MISSED APPROACH: Climb to 2000' via runway heading 248° and outbound LAX VOR R-260 to RAFFS INT and hold.

	ILS				LOC (GS out)					STRAIGHT-IN LANDING RWY 24R
	DH 320'(200')	DH 370'(250')	— MDA 480'(360') With Arbor 1.6 IHQB ILS DME		MDA 620'(500') Without Arbor 1.6 IHQB ILS DME					MDA 620'(500')
	FULL	RAIL or ALS out	MM out	MM out	RAIL out	ALS out		RAIL out	ALS out	ALS out
A	RVR 24 or ½	RVR 40 or ¾	RVR 24 or ½	RVR 24 or ½	RVR 40 or ¾	RVR 50 or 1	RVR 24 or ½	RVR 40 or ¾	RVR 50 or 1	RVR 50 or 1
B							RVR 40 or ¾	RVR 60 or 1¼	RVR 50 or 1	1½
C										
D			RVR 40 or ¾	RVR 40 or ¾	RVR 50 or 1	RVR 60 or 1¼	RVR 60 or 1¼	1¾	1½	2

Gnd speed-Kts	70	90	100	120	140	160
GS 3.00°	377	484	538	646	753	861
ROMEO to MAP 6.2	5:19	4:08	3:43	3:06	2:39	2:20

CHANGES: GS altitudes, minimums.

Q: WHY, ON MANY OCCASIONS AFTER A RELATIVELY SMOOTH FLIGHT, DO A LOT OF BUMPS MATERIALIZE 10 OR 15 MINUTES BEFORE LANDING?

A: The diagram facing shows, in a simplified manner, what has probably taken place. During the enroute phase of your trip you have been flying **above** the clouds, more or less turbulence-free. Upon descent, you must occasionally go through weather fronts closer to the ground. Going in and out of these clouds can produce bumpiness.

Q: WHAT HAPPENS ON AN INSTRUMENT APPROACH IF, AT THE LAST MINUTE, THE CAPTAIN CAN'T SEE THE RUNWAY?

A: Well obviously, if he can't see the ground the pilot has to stay up in the sky. So he will execute what is called a "Missed Approach Procedure." For **every** instrument approach at **every** airport there is a published plan to be followed in the event that the pilot can't land (or sees the ground and decides he doesn't **want** to land for some reason). The captain will have always become familarized with the Missed Approach Procedure in question **before** starting a descent into any airport.

On the top half of the diagram on page 72 there is a heavy **solid** black line leading up from the navigating station for Decatur, Illinois. This is the inbound descent course to the airport, a tiny triangle at the top center of the page. It has three runways. The heavy **broken** line just to the right of the airport shows the Missed Approach Route. Written directly in the **middle** of the diagram are the Missed Approach instructions: "Climbing right turn to 2300 feet. Proceed to the Decatur VOR (navigating station) and go into a holding pattern south of the station."

70

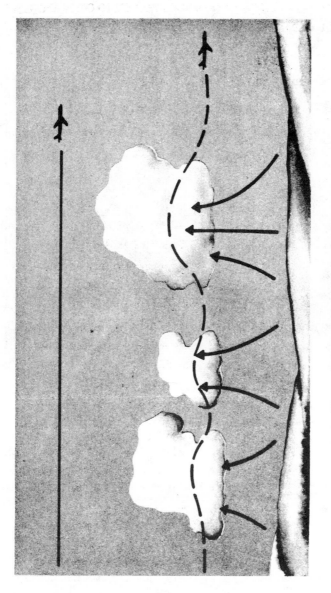

Avoiding turbulence by flying above convective cloud.

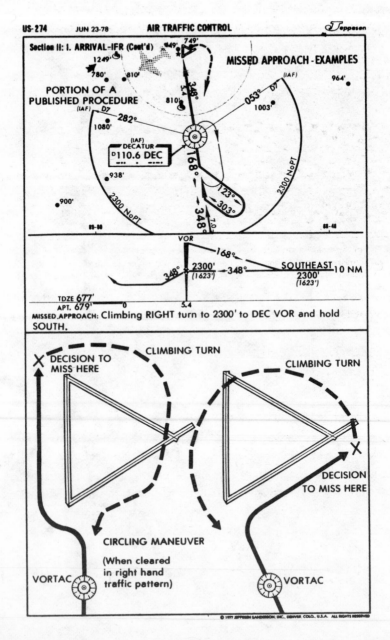

Section II: I. ARRIVAL–IFR (Cont'd)

MISSED APPROACH - EXAMPLES

**PORTION OF A
PUBLISHED PROCEDURE**

DECATUR
D 110.6 DEC

MISSED APPROACH: Climbing RIGHT turn to 2300' to DEC VOR and hold SOUTH.

TDZE 677'
APT. 679'

CLIMBING TURN

DECISION TO
MISS HERE

CLIMBING TURN

DECISION
TO MISS HERE

CIRCLING MANEUVER

(When cleared
in right hand
traffic pattern)

VORTAC

VORTAC

The bottom two diagrams are enlargements of the airport, showing which way the captain will turn depending upon whether he circled the airport from the right or left.

Q: WHERE DOES THE PLANE GO AFTER A MISSED APPROACH?

A: The captain may decide to try again, asking to be vectored around into position by the ground controller for another shot. Or, the plane may proceed to its alternate airport.

Q: A COUPLE OF TIMES WHEN WE'VE COME DOWN THROUGH THE CLOUDS FOR A LANDING WE HAVE BROKEN OUT INTO THE CLEAR— AND RIGHT OFF OUR WING IS ANOTHER BIG JET LANDING ON A PARALLEL RUNWAY. ISN'T THIS CUTTING THINGS A LITTLE CLOSE?

A: A procedure called "Simultaneous Instrument Landing System Approaches" keeps jets apart when using parallel runways. This procedure calls for the vectoring of jets from **opposite** directions before turning to their final straight-in approaches. On the descent, each follows its own individual radio beam, called a "localizer." This signal keeps the planes on a precise course to each runway centerline. There is always a clearly designated "No Transgression Zone" in between the two runways.

This procedure is sometimes used for example, at Los Angeles and Miami airports.

Q: ON A DARK FOGGY NIGHT, OR WHEN THERE'S A BLINDING RAIN OR BLOWING SNOW, HOW DOES THE PILOT KNOW HOW MUCH RUNWAY IS LEFT AFTER HE TOUCHES DOWN?

A: Many airports have what they call "Runway Remaining Lighting." So, lights along the sides of the runway are white until 3,000 feet from the end, when they change to alternating red and white. Then at 1,000 feet from the end, they all turn red.

Q: WITH THE CONTROL TOWER OFTEN LOCATED NEARLY A MILE FROM THE RUNWAY, HOW DO TOWER OPERATORS DETERMINE WHETHER THE JET CAPTAIN CAN SEE THE RUNWAY CLEARLY ENOUGH TO LAND ON A BAD NIGHT?

A: A transmissiometer, an apparatus located alongside the runway, determines prevailing visibility by measuring transmission of light through the atmosphere. The signal is sent by wire to the tower and is read by the controller. This information is given to the pilot. (See diagram on facing page.)

Q: I'VE HEARD ABOUT "WIND SHEAR," ESPECIALLY WHEN A PLANE IS LANDING. WHAT IS IT?

A: Whenever the wind is blowing from several different directions at the same time, or when it radically **changes** direction within a few seconds, you have a "wind shear." It frequently occurs after passage of a thunderstorm near an airport. A certain amount of turbulence is always associated with it.

TRANSMISSIOMETER

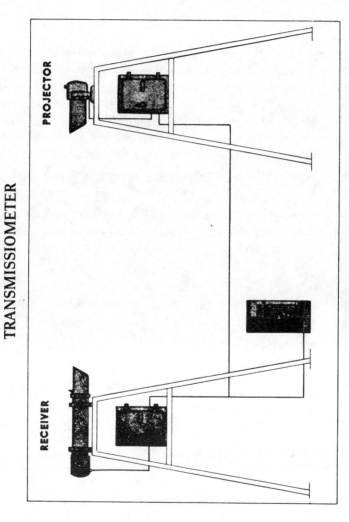

PROJECTOR

RECEIVER

The transmissometer. The projector beams light toward the receiver. Obscuring phenomena in the path of the beam absorbs some of the light. A photoelectric cell in the receiver measures the amount of light penetrating through the obscuring phenomena. The amount received is converted into visibility.

Many devices are now coming into use to help warn the pilot of wind shear. He also receives advisories from the tower and from other pilots who have landed moments before him.

Q: I HATE THOSE STEEP TURNS THE AIRPLANE ALWAYS SEEMS TO MAKE JUST BEFORE WE LAND. WHY ARE THEY NECESSARY?

A: Not every airport has what is called a "straight-in" approach for jetliners. Instead, the plane must make an entrance into a traffic pattern, following it until landing. The first leg of the pattern is called the "downwind." The plane travels parallel to the landing runway but in the **opposite** direction to landing. The first steep turn puts you perpendicular to the runway but at a considerable distance from its threshold. The last steep turn puts the plane onto the final approach and allows it to go "straight in" for touchdown.

Q: WHAT IF THERE IS A POWER FAILURE IN THE CITY WHERE WE ARE LANDING? HOW CAN THE PILOT LAND AT NIGHT WITHOUT RUNWAY LIGHTS?

A: Most airports serving jetliners have emergency generator equipment. It can be activated immediately in the event of a power outage. If this equipment is not available, the pilot will divert to an alternate airport.

Q: ON CERTAIN PLANES I'VE NOTICED A LONG METAL SLAT POP UP FROM THE WING JUST AS WE LAND. WHAT'S THAT FOR?

A: It's called a **speed brake.** In its upright position it interrupts the flow of the air over the wing. This causes the wing to lose most of its lift, not

76

needed any more since you're on the ground, allowing the pilot to use his or her regular foot brakes more effectively.

Q: SOMETIMES RIGHT AFTER LANDING, THE ENGINES SEEM 'TO ROAR UP TO FULL SPEED AGAIN. WHAT'S HAPPENING?

A: Once on the ground the captain reverses the thrust of the jet engines. Instead of air being blown out the **rear** of the engine as in flight, it is now blown out toward the **front** of the engine, causing the plane to slow down.

Q: WHAT HAPPENS IF THE LANDING GEAR WON'T GO DOWN?

A: This occurs very rarely, but if the crew **did** run into this situation it would perform one or more of the emergency gear extension procedures. Since the landing gear of an airliner is very heavy, merely unlocking it will cause it to come down in many cases. On certain jets, the flight engineer can check that the gear is locked into place by the following procedure: he goes back into the cabin, takes a little elevator and descends into the lower galley,opens a tiny window and checks it visually.

In some aircraft there are also systems of prisms or telescopes in the cockpit floor which allow the crew to see the landing gear.

If all other alternatives fail, the Captain will proceed to land with the landing gear up.

Some of the larger airports have facilities to foam the runway, making an easier touchdown. But with or without foam most of the damage is done to the underside of the aircraft—and the pilot's ego.

Q: HOW LONG DOES IT TAKE TO EVACUATE A PLANE?

A: Before an airliner is certified for use by the public the F.A.A. requires an evacuation demonstration **with a full load of passengers which cannot exceed 90 seconds.**

Q: THOSE BIG PLANES MUST BE VERY EXPENSIVE.

A: Very. By the time you read this, the Boeing 747 in your local showroom should be going for more than $30,000,000. But remember. . . with a big down payment, you probably can get generous terms.

Q: HOW MUCH DOES A JET ENGINE COST?

A: It varies with the type of equipment for which it was designed. A single wide-bodied DC-10 jet engine costs around $2,000,000. That's without any accessories.

Q: HOW LONG IS A DC-10 OUT OF SERVICE IF IT HAS TO HAVE AN ENGINE CHANGED?

A: A wing engine on a DC-10 can be removed and another put in its place in less than eight hours. The one in the tail takes longer.

Q: ARE THE JETLINERS OPERATED BY CHARTER COMPANIES AS SAFE AS ONES OPERATED BY THE REGULAR AIRLINES?

A: Yes. Charter pilots are subject to the same exams and check rides as air carrier pilots. Their planes are maintained under identical government regulations.

Q: ARE THERE RULES ABOUT WHO CAN FLY WHERE IN THE AIRSPACE ABOVE THE UNITED STATES?

A: Dozens and dozens of rules. The diagram on the next page lists a few of them. Incidentally, MSL stands for Mean Sea Level (Above Sea Level).

After flight levels add two zeros. For example: FL 290 is the same as 29,000 feet.

MINIMUM VFR VISIBILITY
AND DISTANCE FROM CLOUDS

ALTITUDE	UNCONTROLLED AIRSPACE		CONTROLLED AIRSPACE	
	Flight Visibility	Distance From Clouds	** Flight Visibility	** Distance From Clouds
1200' or less above the surface, regardless of MSL Altitude	*1 statute mile	Clear of clouds	3 statute miles	500' below 1000' above 2000' horizontal
More than 1200' above the surface, but less than 10,000' MSL	1 statute mile	500' below 1000' above 2000' horizontal	3 statute miles	500' below 1000' above 2000' horizontal
More than 1200' above the surface and at or above 10,000' MSL	5 statute miles	1000' below 1000' above 1 statute mile horizontal	5 statute miles	1000' below 1000' above 1 statute mile horizontal

* Helicopters may operate with less than 1 mile visibility, outside controlled airspace at 1200 feet or less above the surface, provided they are operated at a speed that allows the pilot adequate opportunity to see any air traffic or obstructions in time to avoid collisions.

** In addition, when operating within a control zone beneath a ceiling, the ceiling must not be less than 1000'. If the pilot intends to land or takeoff or enter a traffic pattern within a control zone, the ground visibility must be at least 3 miles at that airport. If ground visibility is not reported at the airport, 3 miles flight visibility is required. (FAR 91.105)

ALTITUDES AND FLIGHT LEVELS

CONTROLLED AND UNCONTROLLED AIRSPACE VFR ALTITUDES AND FLIGHT LEVELS			
If your magnetic course (ground track) is	More than 3000' above the surface but below 18,000' MSL fly	Above 18,000' MSL to FL 290 (except within Positive Control Area, FAR 71.193) fly	Above FL 290 (except within Positive Control Area, FAR 71.193) fly 4000' intervals
0° to 179°	Odd thousands, MSL, plus 500' (3500, 5500, 7500, etc)	Odd Flight Levels plus 500' (FL 195, 215, 235, etc)	Beginning at FL 300 (FL 300, 340, 380, etc)
180° to 359°	Even thousands, MSL, plus 500' (4500, 6500, 8500, etc)	Even Flight Levels plus 500' (FL 185, FL 205, 225, etc)	Beginning at FL 320 (FL 320, 360, 400, etc)
UNCONTROLLED AIRSPACE — IFR ALTITUDES AND FLIGHT LEVELS			
If your magnetic course (ground track) is	Below 18,000' MSL, fly	At or above 18,000' MSL but below FL 290, fly	At or above FL 290, fly 4000' intervals
0° to 179°	Odd thousands, MSL, (3000, 5000, 7000, etc)	Odd Flight Levels, FL 190, 210, 230, etc)	Beginning at FL 290, (FL 290, 330, 370, etc)
180° to 359°	Even thousands, MSL, (2000, 4000, 6000, etc)	Even Flight Levels (FL 180, 200, 220, etc)	Beginning at FL 310, (FL 310, 350, 390, etc)

Q: I UNDERSTAND THAT OCCASIONALLY FLIGHT CREWS AND GROUND CONTROLLERS HAVE HAD TROUBLE UNDERSTANDING EACH OTHER'S COMMUNICATIONS. IS THAT TRUE?

A: Not very often. Every instruction issued by a ground controller is repeated back to the controller by a member of the flight crew as a double check.

> CONTROLLER: United 10, climb and maintain flight level three nine zero.

> PILOT: Up to three nine zero. United 10.

Pilots and controllers have a language of their own. See next page for some of it.

Q: HOW DO FOREIGN PILOTS COMMUNICATE WITH THE GROUND IN OUR COUNTRY? HOW DO OUR FLIGHT CREWS MAKE THEMSELVES UNDERSTOOD ABROAD?

A: English is the international language for all intercontinental flights. All pilots flying these routes, and all controllers operating the ground stations, must be fluent in English in every country where the big passenger jets operate.

Section II: C. RADIO COMMUNICATIONS PHRASEOLOGY AND TECHNIQUES

PHONETIC ALPHABET

LETTER	CODE	WORD	LATIN ALPHABET REPRESENTATION
A	• —	Alfa	AL FAH
B	— • • •	Bravo	BRAH VOH
C	— • — •	Charlie	CHAR LEE or
			SHAR LEE
D	— • •	Delta	DELL TAH
E	•	Echo	ECK OH
F	• • — •	Foxtrot	FOKS TROT
G	— — •	Golf	GOLF
H	• • • •	Hotel	HOH TELL
I	• •	India	IN DEE AH
J	• — — —	Juliett	JEW LEE ETT
K	— • —	Kilo	KEY LOH
L	• — • •	Lima	LEE MAH
M	— —	Mike	MIKE
N	— •	November	NO VEM BER
O	— — —	Oscar	OSS CAH
P	• — — •	Papa	PAH PAH
Q	— — • —	Quebec	KEH BECK
R	• — •	Romeo	ROW ME OH
S	• • •	Sierra	SEE AIR RAH
T	—	Tango	TANG GO
U	• • —	Uniform	YOU NEE FORM or
			OO NEE FORM
V	• • • —	Victor	VIK TAH
W	• — —	Whiskey	WISS KEY
X	— • • —	X-ray	ECKS RAY
Y	— • — —	Yankee	YANG KEY
Z	— — • •	Zulu	ZOO LOO

NUMERAL OR NUMERAL ELEMENT	CODE	PRONUNCIATION
1	• — — — —	WUN
2	• • — — —	TOO
3	• • • — —	TREE
4	• • • • —	FOW-er
5	• • • • •	FIFE
6	— • • • •	SIX
7	— — • • •	SEV-en
8	— — — • •	AIT
9	— — — — •	NIN-er
0	— — — — —	ZE-RO
Decimal		DAY-SEE-MAL
Thousand		TOU-SAND

Q: ALTHOUGH I'VE WORRIED ABOUT THE POSSIBILITY, I'VE NEVER SEEN ICE ON THE WINGS OF AN AIRLINER.

A: And, you probably never will. There are heating elements all over the big jets to keep them from icing up.

Q: IS THERE A WAY I COULD LISTEN TO AVIATION WEATHER FORECASTS IN MY AREA?

A: Sure, but you'll have to get a radio with a low frequency band. On the next page is a map showing all the weather broadcasting stations operated across the country by the F.A.A.. These stations constantly relay information which applies primarily to flight conditions.

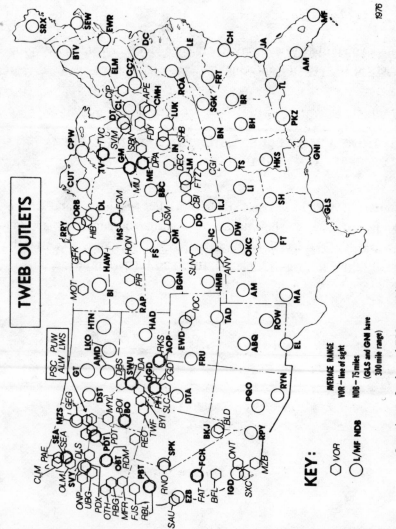

TWEB OUTLETS

KEY:

⬡ VOR

◯ L/MF NDB

AVERAGE RANGE
VOR — line of sight
NDB — 75 miles
(GLS and GNI have 300 mile range)

Locations of selected FSSs providing Transcribed Weather Broadcasts (TWEBs).

1976

Q: WHERE CAN A PILOT EXPECT THE LARGEST NUMBER OF THUNDERSTORMS EACH YEAR?

A: See diagram on next page.

Q: DON'T THE DIFFERENT TEMPERATURES AT AIRPORTS AROUND THE WORLD CREATE LOTS OF PROBLEMS FOR JET ENGINES?

A: The surface temperatures from place to place don't vary that much, as you can see from the diagram on page 88. However, the temperature differences between the **surface** of the earth and the **altitudes** at which jets fly are enormous. It may be **60 below zero** outside the cabin while you're cruising along and **90 above zero** when you land.

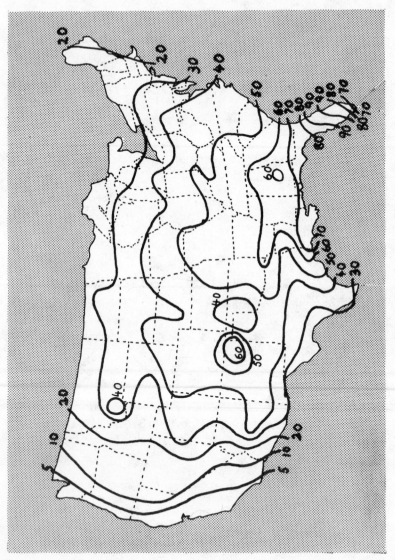

The average number of thunderstorms each year.

Jet engines have been designed to withstand almost every conceivable temperature change.

Q: I'VE HEARD THAT U.S. MILITARY FIGHTER PLANES SOMETIMES USE AIRLINERS AS "TARGETS" AND INTERCEPT THEM. IS THAT TRUE?

A: Not so far as I can determine.

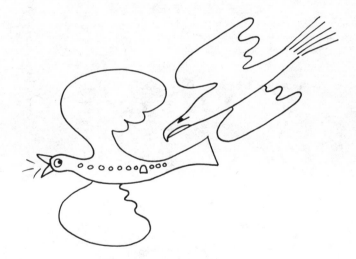

Q: DOES THE PILOT HAVE TO DO WHATEVER THE GROUND CONTROLLERS TELL HIM?

A: The pilot is expected to follow the instructions of the ground controllers. However, the captain is the captain so he may deviate from any instruction that he decides would endanger his flight.

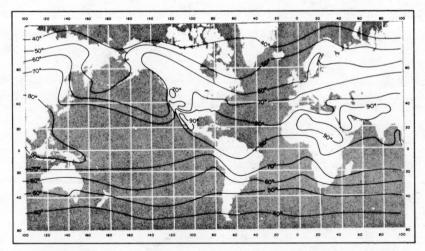

World-wide average surface temperatures in July. In the Northern Hemisphere, continents generally are warmer than oceanic areas at corresponding latitudes. The reverse is true in the Southern Hemisphere, but the contrast is not so evident because of the sparcity of land surfaces.

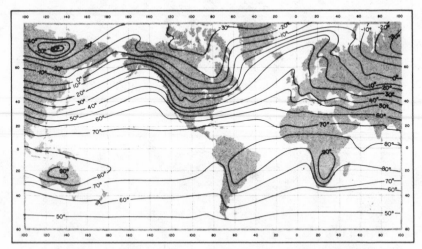

World-wide average surface temperatures in January when the Northern Hemisphere is in the cold season and the Southern Hemisphere is warm. Note that in the Northern Hemisphere, continents are colder than the oceanic areas at corresponding latitudes, and in the Southern Hemisphere continents are warmer than oceans.

Q: IS IT TRUE THAT EVERY WORD SPOKEN IN A JETLINER COCKPIT IS RECORDED?

A: Yes. Also, all communications between the plane and control towers and ground controllers are recorded.

Q: HOW LONG ARE THE RECORDINGS KEPT?

A: Usually for 90 days.

Q: HOW LONG WOULD A 747 FLOAT IF IT DITCHED IN THE OCEAN?

A: 747s are supposed to float long enough to get everyone out of the cabins and into life rafts. However, in the almost 20 years they've been flying, no passenger jet has had to ditch in mid-ocean.

Q: DO FLIGHT CREWS CARRY FIREARMS?

A: No.

Q: WHY DO THERE SEEM TO BE SO MANY ACCIDENTS INVOLVING LITTLE PLANES?

A: For one thing, there are many more small planes than airliners. General aviation (light planes) comprises 98% of the civil aircraft in the United States. Light planes have 96% of the pilots, fly more than 84% of all civil aircraft hours and 61% of plane miles (34,000,000 hours annually vs. 6,000,000 for airlines). They cover 4.2 billion miles a year to the airlines' 2.6 billion, transport 100 million persons a year (one of every three air travelers), and encompass every form of aviation activity from carrying mail to planting rice crops.

Q: ARE THERE ANY WOMEN AIRLINE PILOTS FLYING TODAY?

A: Just a handful. Most are co-pilots.

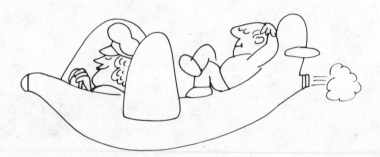

Q: WHY IS THAT? AREN'T THEY CAPABLE OF BEING CAPTAINS?

A: Given the same training and experience levels, female pilots are just as capable as male pilots. Flying an airliner doesn't demand any kind of super strength. But it requires years and years of working one's way up through the ranks. Women weren't given that opportunity until fairly recently.

Rest assured if one day you have a female captain flying up there in the left seat, she'll be every bit as good as her male counterpart. Many of aviation's records have been established and broken by women pilots.

Q: HOW OFTEN MUST AIRLINE PILOTS TAKE A PHYSICAL EXAMINATION?

A: A pilot with an Air Transport Rating must have a physical every six months.

Q: IS THERE A MANDATORY RETIREMENT AGE FOR PILOTS?

A: Yes. A pilot must retire on his 60th birthday. (There is currently some talk of raising this.)

Q: WHAT KIND OF GASOLINE DO THEY BURN IN AIRLINERS?

A: They don't burn gasoline. Instead they use something called (appropriately) **jet fuel**. It has a lot of kerosene in it and comes in several different grades (just like at your corner gas station).

Q: WHAT IF ALL THE INSTRUMENTS IN THE COCKPIT OF AN AIR LINER SUDDENLY BECAME USELESS? IS THAT THE END?

A: It takes a long stretch of a vivid imagination to plot a scenario to accommodate that possibility. Most cockpit instruments have backups. Some have backups for the backups. In any event, to land the plane safely in half-way decent weather a pilot really only needs an instrument called an **attitude indicator** plus his airspeed indicator. The attitude indicator on an airliner has several backups.

Q: WHAT IF THERE SHOULD BE A TOTAL POWER FAILURE ON A PLANE?

A: On a 747, for example, one of the attitude indicators has its own **independent** power source, so that it will function no matter what. The

airspeed indicator needs no power source because it runs off air
pressure from outside.

Q: **WHY DO SOME CAPTAINS TALK SO MUCH ON THE PUBLIC
ADDRESS SYSTEM?**

A: Just ignore those types. Be glad they know where their airplane is at
all times.

Q: **HOW CAN I BE SURE THEY KNOW?**

A: They know.

Q: **COULD THE CAPTAIN OF AN AIRLINER PERFORM A MARRIAGE
CEREMONY?**

A: Why don't you wait until the plane lands?

Q: **WHY DO YOU THINK SO MANY PEOPLE ARE NERVOUS
ABOUT FLYING?**

A: Obviously, there are many answers to this question. Only trained
experts should be consulted if you want to investigate it in any depth.
However, one thing is quite obvious: an airline passenger seated in the

plane's cabin is totally **out of control of the situation.** In a car, one can pull over to the side and stop, speed up, turn left, go home, whatever. In an airliner, a passenger can't do any of these things - or even see the people who are doing them.

Being unable to have an influence over one's destiny in an airliner **must** be bothersome to certain individuals. However, there shouldn't be a shadow of doubt that the crew is able to handle things better than a passenger can. A **lot** better. How about a **million times better**?

Also, never forget what I told you before: MORE THAN 99.9999% OF ALL AIRLINE FLIGHTS ARE COMPLETED SAFELY. GO FIND BETTER ODDS ON **ANYTHING** ANYWHERE ELSE.

ABOUT THE AUTHOR

Perry Lafferty has spent all of his professional life in radio and television. During the past 25 years he has produced and/or directed nearly 1,000 television shows, in addition to having served a 10-year hitch as vice president in charge of programs for CBS Television in Los Angeles.

When in his 50s he decided to pursue an interest he had developed during his many years of jetting back and forth between Los Angeles and New York on TV assignments — namely **flying**. Up to this point his knowledge of life from the ground to 35,000 feet was more or less that of the average person.

He made Santa Monica Airport in California his home base and, in whatever spare time he could muster, he was airborne. Today he holds a Commercial Pilot Certificate for single and multi-engine land planes, an instrument rating, a ground instructor rating and two flight instructor ratings. One of the latter allows him to teach people to fly; the other permits him to instruct people how to do so solely by instruments.

Mr. Lafferty is currently Senior Vice President for Programs and Talent at NBC Entertainment in Burbank, California.

This book is published by

PRICE/STERN/SLOAN
Publishers, Inc., Los Angeles

publishers of

HOW TO REACH ANYONE WHO'S ANYONE ($4.95)

TRAPPED IN THE ORGANIZATION ($2.50)

MURPHY'S LAW AND OTHER REASONS WHY
THINGS GO ⅃NOᴙW! ($2.50)

MURPHY'S LAW / BOOK TWO ($2.50)

HOW TO FLATTEN YOUR STOMACH ($1.75)

HOW TO TRIM YOUR HIPS AND
SHAPE YOUR THIGHS ($1.75)

COACH JIM EVERROAD'S 5-MINUTE
TOTAL SHAPE-UP PROGRAM ($1.75)

and many, many more

They are available wherever books are sold, or may be
ordered directly from the publisher by sending a check
or money order for total amount plus 50 cents for handling
and mailing. For a complete list of tiles send a
stamped, self addressed envelope to:

PRICE/STERN/SLOAN *Publishers, Inc.*
410 North La Cienega Boulevard, Los Angeles, California 90048